# JUICING

## FOR

## PANCREATIC CANCER
## REVERSAL

Quick and easy nutrient-rich juice and smoothie recipes
that you can make at home to help you fight and treat
pancreatic cancer effectively

Dr. Victoria Sterling

# TABLE OF CONTENTS

INTRODUCTION _____ 5

❖ **What is Pancreatic Cancer?** _____ 8

❖ **Causes of Pancreatic Cancer:** _____ 8

❖ **Symptoms of Pancreatic Cancer:** _____ 9

❖ **Preventive Measures:** _____ 10

❖ **Selecting the Perfect Juicer** _____ 12

❖ **Selecting the Right Produce** _____ 15

HEALING JUICE AND SMOOTHIE RECIPES _____ 19

1. Immune Booster Juice _____ 19
2. Carrot-Ginger Elixir _____ 20
3. Beetroot-Orange Vitality Juice _____ 21
4. Green Energy Kick _____ 22
5. Anti-Inflammatory Turmeric Juice _____ 23
6. Berry-licious Antioxidant Juice _____ 24
7. Green Superfood Smoothie _____ 25
8. Creamy Turmeric Delight _____ 26
9. Protein-Packed Green Smoothie _____ 27
10. Digestive Soother _____ 28
11. Avocado-Berry Bliss _____ 29
12. Golden Mango-Turmeric Smoothie _____ 30
13. Nutty Banana-Spinach Smoothie _____ 31

14. Citrus-Berry Zest Smoothie _____ 32

15. Pineapple-Kale Euphoria _____ 33

16. Papaya-Coconut Dream_____ 34

17. Blueberry-Chia Powerhouse _____ 35

18. Watermelon-Cucumber Cooler _____ 36

19. Peach-Raspberry Delight _____ 37

20. Kiwi-Strawberry Surprise_____ 38

21. Green Detox Smoothie                                              39

22. Blueberry-Kale Revitalizer _____ 40

23. Papaya-Coconut Bliss_____ 41

24. Citrus-Berry Burst _____ 42

25. Pineapple-Spinach Wonder _____ 43

26. Almond Butter-Banana Smoothie _____ 44

27. Papaya-Pineapple Paradise _____ 45

28. Chia-Berry Antioxidant Smoothie _____ 46

29. Kiwi-Mango Delight _____ 47

CONCLUSION _____**49**

# INTRODUCTION

Friends, I am Dr. Victoria Sterling, and I want to share an incredible journey with you - one that centers on the power of nutrient-rich juices and smoothies in the fight against pancreatic cancer.

Not too long ago, I met a remarkable man named John. His life took a heart-wrenching turn when he was diagnosed with pancreatic cancer. As you can imagine, the news was devastating for him and his loved ones. His days that were once filled with the joys of life suddenly became inundated with medical appointments, tests, and an overwhelming fear of the uncertain path ahead.

But John was a fighter, and he refused to surrender without a battle. That's when he stumbled upon my name, Dr. Victoria Sterling, a nutritionist with years of experience and a passion for helping those in need.

With courage and trembling hands, John dialed my number, and I remember that phone call like it was yesterday. His voice was filled with trepidation, but there was also a glimmer of hope in the way he spoke. As I listened to his fears and hopes, I knew I had to do everything in my power to help him.

With unwavering determination, I embarked on a mission to assist John. The road to recovery was far from smooth, but I firmly believed in the potential of nutrient-rich juices and smoothies. I knew that they could make a difference, and I was determined to prove it.

John's kitchen transformed into a sanctuary of hope, filled with colorful fruits and vegetables. I provided him with a list of ingredients and simple, yet effective, recipes for nutrient-rich juice and smoothie blends. The aroma and vivid hues that emanated from his kitchen were like a promise of vitality and health.

Every day, John faithfully sipped on the concoctions I had designed, tailored to support his body in its battle against pancreatic cancer. As he persisted with this routine, he began to notice subtle changes – his energy levels increased, his strength was restored, and a newfound optimism bloomed within him.

Months went by, and the day of John's next check-up arrived. As he sat nervously in the waiting room, there was a distinct sense of hope in his eyes that was undeniable. The doctor reviewed his reports, and then, a smile spread across his face that spoke of disbelief.

"Your tumor has shrunk," the doctor stated in awe.

It was the result of the incredible impact of the nutrient-rich blends I had recommended.

John's determination, combined with my unwavering support, had made the impossible a reality. The tumor continued to shrink until it was nothing more than a distant memory.

Today, John lives a vibrant life, enveloped in the love of his family and brimming with gratitude. His journey, from a diagnosis that felt like a death sentence to a life filled with hope and health, is a testament to the power of my expertise and the miracle of nutrient-rich juice and smoothie blends.

This is just the beginning of a remarkable journey, one that you too can embark upon. In **"Juicing for Pancreatic Cancer Reversal"**, I share the very recipes and knowledge that transformed John's life. If you or a loved one is facing the daunting battle against pancreatic cancer, this book is the guiding light that can lead you towards a path of healing, health, and hope.

# What is Pancreatic Cancer?

Pancreatic cancer is a malignant disease that originates in the pancreas, a vital organ located behind the stomach. The pancreas has two main functions: it produces digestive enzymes to help break down food and plays a crucial role in regulating blood sugar levels by producing insulin and other hormones. Pancreatic cancer occurs when cells within the pancreas start to grow uncontrollably, forming a tumor. It is a particularly aggressive and challenging form of cancer due to its often late-stage diagnosis and limited treatment options.

## Causes of Pancreatic Cancer:

The exact cause of pancreatic cancer is not always clear, but several risk factors have been identified:

Tobacco Use: Smoking is one of the most significant risk factors for pancreatic cancer. Smokers are at a higher risk compared to non-smokers.

Age: The risk of pancreatic cancer increases with age, with most cases occurring in people over the age of 45.

**Family History:** A family history of pancreatic cancer or certain genetic mutations can increase the risk of developing the disease.

**Chronic Pancreatitis:** Long-term inflammation of the pancreas, often caused by excessive alcohol consumption, can increase the risk.

**Obesity:** Being overweight or obese has been associated with a higher risk of pancreatic cancer.

**Diabetes:** Long-standing diabetes can be both a risk factor and an early symptom of pancreatic cancer.

## Symptoms of Pancreatic Cancer:

Pancreatic cancer is known as a **"silent"** disease because it often remains asymptomatic until it reaches an advanced stage. Common symptoms may include:

**Jaundice:** Yellowing of the skin and eyes due to a blocked bile duct.

**Abdominal Pain:** Dull aching pain that may radiate to the back.

**Unintended Weight Loss:** A significant and unexplained loss of weight.

**Appetite Loss:** A reduced desire to eat.

**Changes in Stool:** Light-colored or greasy stools, possibly with an unusual odor.

**New-Onset Diabetes:** Especially in older adults, diabetes may develop without an obvious cause.

**Digestive Problems:** Nausea, vomiting, and diarrhea.

## Preventive Measures:

While there is no surefire way to prevent pancreatic cancer, there are steps you can take to reduce your risk:

**Quit Smoking:** If you smoke, quitting is one of the most effective ways to lower your risk.

**Maintain a Healthy Weight:** Staying within a healthy weight range through a balanced diet and regular physical activity can reduce your risk.

**Limit Alcohol Consumption:** Moderation in alcohol consumption is advised to reduce the risk of chronic pancreatitis.

**Manage Diabetes:** If you have diabetes, work with your healthcare provider to manage it effectively.

**Screening for High-Risk Individuals:** Those with a family history of pancreatic cancer or certain genetic mutations may benefit from regular screenings and monitoring.

**Healthy Diet:** Incorporating a diet rich in fruits, vegetables, and whole grains may be beneficial.

**Stay Informed:** Be aware of the risk factors, symptoms, and early detection methods to seek prompt medical attention if you suspect any issues.

In summary, pancreatic cancer is a challenging disease with limited early detection methods, which is why understanding the risk factors and potential symptoms is vital. By making healthy lifestyle choices and staying vigilant, you can reduce your risk and potentially catch the disease at an earlier, more treatable stage.

Selecting the Perfect Juicer for Juice and Smoothies in Pancreatic Cancer Treatment

When considering a juicer for making nutritious juices and smoothies as part of your pancreatic cancer treatment plan, it's important to choose the right one to maximize the health benefits. Here are some tips to help you select the perfect juicer:

## 1. Type of Juicer:

**Centrifugal Juicers:** These are common and budget-friendly, but they may not extract as much juice and nutrients from fruits and vegetables. They work well for basic juice but may not be ideal for pancreatic cancer treatment.

**Masticating Juicers:** These slow, cold-press juicers are often preferred for cancer patients. They preserve more nutrients and enzymes, making them a better choice for therapeutic juices and smoothies.

**Blenders:** While not technically a juicer, blenders are excellent for making smoothies, which retain the fiber from fruits and vegetables. Blended smoothies can be a valuable addition to a cancer treatment diet.

## 2. Nutrient Retention:

Look for a juicer that minimizes heat and oxidation during the juicing process. This helps preserve the essential nutrients and enzymes in the juice, which is crucial for pancreatic cancer patients.

## 3. Ease of Cleaning:

A juicer that is easy to disassemble and clean will encourage you to use it regularly. Convenience matters, especially during treatment when energy levels can be low.

## 4. Yield and Pulp:

Consider how much juice the juicer extracts from the ingredients. Less waste in the pulp container means more value for your ingredients.

## 5. Size and Noise:

Ensure the juicer fits your kitchen and lifestyle. If you have a small kitchen, opt for a compact model. Additionally, consider the noise level, especially if you plan to juice early in the morning or late at night.

## 6. Durability:

Look for a juicer with a strong and durable build. Cancer treatment might require long-term use of the juicer, so it's essential that it can withstand regular use.

## 7. Price:

Determine your budget but also keep in mind that a good-quality juicer can be an investment in your health. It's often worth spending a bit more for a juicer that meets your needs and offers durability.

## 8. BPA-Free Materials:

Ensure that the juicer's components, particularly those that come into contact with the juice, are made from BPA-free materials to avoid potential chemical contamination.

## 9. Safety Features:

Look for safety features like overload protection and automatic shutoff in case of overheating. Safety is crucial, especially if you plan to use the juicer during your treatment.

Ultimately, the perfect juicer for pancreatic cancer treatment is one that suits your specific needs, lifestyle, and dietary preferences.

Selecting the Right Produce for Juicing and Smoothies in Pancreatic Cancer Treatment

When you're incorporating juicing and smoothies into your pancreatic cancer treatment plan, choosing the right produce is crucial for ensuring maximum nutritional benefits. Here are some tips to help you select the right ingredients:

### 1. Freshness and Quality:

Opt for fresh, high-quality produce. Look for fruits and vegetables that are firm, vibrant in color, and free from bruises or blemishes. Fresh produce contains more nutrients.

### 2. Variety is Key:

Aim for a diverse selection of fruits and vegetables to obtain a wide range of essential nutrients. Different colors indicate different types of phytonutrients, so choose a variety of colors.

### 3. Organic vs. Conventional:

Consider choosing organic produce, especially for items on the Environmental Working Group's "Dirty Dozen" list, which identifies produce with higher pesticide residues. Organic options reduce your exposure to potentially harmful chemicals.

### 4. Seasonal Produce:

Incorporate seasonal produce into your juices and smoothies. Seasonal fruits and vegetables are typically fresher, more flavorful, and may be more affordable.

### 5. Leafy Greens:

Leafy greens like kale, spinach, and Swiss chard are packed with vitamins, minerals, and antioxidants. They're excellent additions to your juices and smoothies.

### 6. Cruciferous Vegetables:

Vegetables like broccoli, cauliflower, and Brussels sprouts contain compounds that may have cancer-fighting properties. Include them in your recipes.

### 7. Berries:

Berries like blueberries, strawberries, and raspberries are rich in antioxidants. They can help reduce oxidative stress and inflammation, which are important in cancer management.

### 8. Citrus Fruits:

Citrus fruits such as oranges, lemons, and grapefruits provide vitamin C and other beneficial compounds that support the immune system.

## 9. Ginger and Turmeric:

Both ginger and turmeric have anti-inflammatory properties. They can add flavor and therapeutic benefits to your concoctions.

## 10. Herbs and Spices:

Fresh herbs like parsley and mint, and spices like cinnamon and nutmeg, can enhance the flavor and health benefits of your drinks.

## 11. Avocado:

Avocado can add creaminess to smoothies and provide healthy fats and fiber.

## 12. Be Mindful of Sugar Content:

Limit the use of high-sugar fruits like pineapples and mangos. Opt for low-sugar options like berries and green apples, or use them in moderation.

## 13. Wash Thoroughly:

Wash all produce, even if it's organic, to remove dirt, pesticides, and potential contaminants.

## 15. Portion Control:

Be mindful of portion sizes. A well-balanced juice or smoothie should include a variety of ingredients but not be overly large.

# HEALING JUICE AND SMOOTHIE RECIPES

## 1. Immune Booster Juice

**Ingredients:**

- 1 cup spinach
- 1/2 cucumber
- 1 green apple

**Preparation:**

Wash the ingredients and juice them together.

**Servings:** 1

**Nutritional Value:** High in vitamins, minerals, and antioxidants.

**Cooking Time:** 5 minutes

## 2. Carrot-Ginger Elixir

**Ingredients:**

- 4 carrots
- 1-inch piece of fresh ginger

**Preparation:**

Wash and peel the carrots and ginger, then juice them.

**Servings:** 1

**Nutritional Value:** Rich in antioxidants and anti-inflammatory properties.

**Cooking Time:** 5 minutes

# 3. Beetroot-Orange Vitality Juice

**Ingredients:**

- 1 beetroot
- 2 oranges

**Preparation:**

Wash, peel, and juice the beetroot and oranges.

**Servings:** 1

**Nutritional Value:** High in vitamin C, fiber, and antioxidants.

**Cooking Time:** 5 minutes

# 4. Green Energy Kick

**Ingredients:**

- 2 cups kale
- 1 green apple
- 1 lemon (peeled)

**Preparation:**

Wash and juice the ingredients.

**Servings:** 1

**Nutritional Value:** Abundant in vitamins, minerals, and chlorophyll.

**Cooking Time:** 5 minutes

# 5. Anti-Inflammatory Turmeric Juice

**Ingredients:**

- 1-inch piece of turmeric
- 2 carrots
- 1 orange

**Preparation:**

Wash, peel, and juice the ingredients.

**Servings:** 1

**Nutritional Value:** High in anti-inflammatory and antioxidant compounds.

**Cooking Time:** 5 minutes

# 6. Berry-licious Antioxidant Juice

**Ingredients:**

- 1 cup mixed berries (blueberries, strawberries, raspberries)
- 1 green apple

**Preparation:**

Wash the fruits and juice them together.

**Servings:** 1

**Nutritional Value:** Rich in antioxidants, vitamins, and fiber.

**Cooking Time:** 5 minutes

**Ingredients:**

- 2 cups spinach
- 1/2 avocado
- 1 banana
- 1 cup almond milk (unsweetened)

**Preparation:**

Blend all the ingredients until smooth.

**Servings:** 1

**Nutritional Value:** High in vitamins, minerals, healthy fats, and fiber.

**Cooking Time:** 5 minutes

# 8. Creamy Turmeric Delight

## Ingredients:

- 1 teaspoon turmeric
- 1/2 cup Greek yogurt (plain)
- 1/2 banana
- 1/2 cup coconut milk (unsweetened)

## Preparation:

Blend all ingredients until smooth.

**Servings:** 1

**Nutritional Value:** Anti-inflammatory properties, probiotics, and healthy fats.

**Cooking Time:** 5 minutes

# 9. Protein-Packed Green Smoothie

**Ingredients:**

- 2 cups kale
- 1 scoop of plant-based protein powder
- 1/2 avocado
- 1/2 cup almond milk (unsweetened)

**Preparation:**

Blend all ingredients until smooth.

**Servings:** 1

**Nutritional Value:** High in protein, vitamins, minerals, and healthy fats.

**Cooking Time:** 5 minutes

# 10. Digestive Soother

**Ingredients:**

- 1/2 cup papaya
- 1/2 cup pineapple
- 1/2 cup Greek yogurt (plain)

**Preparation:**

Blend all ingredients until smooth.

**Servings:** 1

**Nutritional Value:** Enzymes for digestion and probiotics.

**Cooking Time:** 5 minutes

# 11. Avocado-Berry Bliss

**Ingredients:**

- 1/2 avocado
- 1 cup mixed berries (blueberries, strawberries, raspberries)
- 1 cup coconut water (unsweetened)

**Preparation:**

Blend all ingredients until smooth.

**Servings:** 1

**Nutritional Value:** Healthy fats, antioxidants, and hydration.

**Cooking Time:** 5 minutes

**Ingredients:**

- 1 cup mango (frozen)
- 1/2 teaspoon turmeric
- 1/2 cup almond milk (unsweetened)

**Preparation:**

Blend all ingredients until smooth.

**Servings:** 1

**Nutritional Value:** Anti-inflammatory properties, vitamins, and minerals.

**Cooking Time:** 5 minutes

**Ingredients:**

- 1 banana
- 2 cups spinach
- 1 tablespoon almond butter
- 1 cup almond milk (unsweetened)

**Preparation:**

Blend all ingredients until smooth.

**Servings:** 1

**Nutritional Value:** Vitamins, minerals, healthy fats, and fiber.

**Cooking Time:** 5 minutes

# 14. Citrus-Berry Zest Smoothie

**Ingredients:**

- 1 orange (peeled)
- 1 cup mixed berries (blueberries, strawberries, raspberries)
- 1/2 cup Greek yogurt (plain)

**Preparation:**

Blend all ingredients until smooth.

**Servings:** 1

**Nutritional Value:** Vitamin C, antioxidants, and probiotics.

**Cooking Time:** 5 minutes

# 15. Pineapple-Kale Euphoria

**Ingredients:**

- 1 cup pineapple
- 2 cups kale
- 1/2 cucumber

**Preparation:**

Blend all ingredients until smooth.

**Servings:** 1

**Nutritional Value:** Vitamins, minerals, antioxidants, and hydration.

**Cooking Time:** 5 minutes

# 16. Papaya-Coconut Dream

**Ingredients:**

- 1 cup papaya
- 1/2 cup coconut milk (unsweetened)
- 1/2 cup Greek yogurt (plain)

**Preparation:**

Blend all ingredients until smooth.

**Servings:** 1

**Nutritional Value:** Digestive enzymes, probiotics, and healthy fats.

**Cooking Time:** 5 minutes

## 17. Blueberry-Chia Powerhouse

**Ingredients:**

- 1 cup blueberries
- 1 tablespoon chia seeds
- 1/2 cup almond milk (unsweetened)

**Preparation:**

Blend all ingredients except chia seeds until smooth. Stir in chia seeds after blending.

**Servings:** 1

**Nutritional Value:** Antioxidants, omega-3 fatty acids, and fiber.

**Cooking Time:** 5 minutes

**Ingredients:**

- 1 cup watermelon
- 1/2 cucumber
- 1 lime (juiced)

**Preparation:**

Blend all ingredients until smooth.

**Servings:** 1

**Nutritional Value:** Hydration, vitamins, and minerals.

**Cooking Time:** 5 minutes

# 19. Peach-Raspberry Delight

## Ingredients:

- 1 cup peaches (frozen)
- 1/2 cup raspberries
- 1/2 cup Greek yogurt (plain)

## Preparation:

Blend all ingredients until smooth.

**Servings:** 1

**Nutritional Value:** Antioxidants, probiotics, and vitamins.

**Cooking Time:** 5 minutes

# 20. Kiwi-Strawberry Surprise

**Ingredients:**

- 2 kiwis
- 1 cup strawberries
- 1/2 cup almond milk (unsweetened)

**Preparation:**

Blend all ingredients until smooth.

**Servings:** 1

**Nutritional Value:** Vitamin C, fiber, and antioxidants.

**Cooking Time:** 5 minutes

**Ingredients:**

- 2 cups spinach
- 1/2 cucumber
- 1 green apple
- 1/2 lemon (juiced)

**Preparation:**

Blend all ingredients until smooth.

**Servings:** 1

**Nutritional Value:** Detoxifying properties, vitamins, and minerals.

**Cooking Time:** 5 minutes

## 22. Blueberry-Kale Revitalizer

**Ingredients:**

- 1 cup blueberries
- 2 cups kale
- 1/2 banana
- 1/2 cup almond milk (unsweetened)

**Preparation:**

Blend all ingredients until smooth.

**Servings:** 1

**Nutritional Value:** Antioxidants, vitamins, minerals, and fiber.

**Cooking Time:** 5 minutes

**Ingredients:**

- 1 cup papaya
- 1/2 cup coconut milk (unsweetened)
- 1/2 banana

**Preparation:**

Blend all ingredients until smooth.

**Servings:** 1

**Nutritional Value:** Digestive enzymes, healthy fats, and vitamins.

**Cooking Time:** 5 minutes

**Ingredients:**

- 1 orange (peeled)
- 1 cup mixed berries (blueberries, strawberries, raspberries)
- 1/2 cup almond milk (unsweetened)

**Preparation:**

Blend all ingredients until smooth.

**Servings:** 1

**Nutritional Value:** Vitamin C, antioxidants, and fiber.

**Cooking Time:** 5 minutes

## 25. Pineapple-Spinach Wonder

**Ingredients:**

- 1 cup pineapple
- 2 cups spinach
- 1/2 banana
- 1/2 cup almond milk (unsweetened)

**Preparation:**

Blend all ingredients until smooth.

**Servings:** 1

**Nutritional Value:** Vitamins, minerals, antioxidants, and hydration.

**Cooking Time:** 5 minutes

# 26. Almond Butter-Banana Smoothie

**Ingredients:**

- 1 banana
- 1 tablespoon almond butter
- 1/2 cup almond milk (unsweetened)

**Preparation:**

Blend all ingredients until smooth.

**Servings:** 1

**Nutritional Value:** Healthy fats, vitamins, minerals, and fiber.

**Cooking Time:** 5 minutes

# 27. Papaya-Pineapple Paradise

**Ingredients:**

- 1 cup papaya
- 1 cup pineapple
- 1/2 cup coconut water (unsweetened)

**Preparation:**

Blend all ingredients until smooth.

**Servings:** 1

**Nutritional Value:** Digestive enzymes, vitamins, minerals, and hydration.

**Cooking Time:** 5 minutes

# 28. Chia-Berry Antioxidant Smoothie

Ingredients:

- 1 cup mixed berries (blueberries, strawberries, raspberries)
- 1 tablespoon chia seeds
- 1/2 cup almond milk (unsweetened)

**Preparation:**

Blend all ingredients except chia seeds until smooth. Stir in chia seeds after blending.

**Servings:** 1

**Nutritional Value:** Antioxidants, omega-3 fatty acids, and fiber.

**Cooking Time:** 5 minutes

**Ingredients:**

- 2 kiwis
- 1 cup mango (frozen)
- 1/2 cup almond milk (unsweetened)

**Preparation:**

Blend all ingredients until smooth.

**Servings**: 1

**Nutritional Value:** Vitamin C, fiber, and antioxidants.

**Cooking Time:** 5 minutes

These 30 recipes are designed to provide a variety of flavors and health benefits while adhering to your dietary restrictions. Remember to consult with your healthcare provider or nutritionist to ensure these recipes align with your specific treatment plan. Enjoy your journey to better health with these delicious and nutritious juices and smoothies.

# CONCLUSION

In the journey toward pancreatic cancer reversal, the importance of nourishment cannot be overstated. Throughout this exploration of juicing and smoothie recipes tailored to combat this relentless adversary, we've uncovered the immense potential that lies within the vibrant, natural ingredients. These elixirs, concocted with precision and love, have the power to infuse your body with vitality, hope, and strength.

We've delved into the world of fresh, high-quality produce, selecting ingredients that are not just delicious, but scientifically proven to assist in your battle against pancreatic cancer. From the verdant greens to the vibrant berries and the anti-inflammatory spices, each recipe carries a purpose beyond mere flavor; it is your armor, your fortification, your means to foster healing.

In closing, I implore you to embrace these recipes as a lifeline, a source of resilience and rejuvenation. The journey to recovery may be arduous, but it is also a journey of transformation. Your body is an incredible vessel, and within it lies an indomitable spirit.

By nurturing it with these nutrient-rich blends, you are taking the first step toward reclaiming your life, your health, and your future.

Remember, this is not just a book; it is a promise of renewal. It is a testament to the strength of the human spirit and the power of nature's bounty. The road to recovery may have its challenges, but you are not alone. You have the wisdom of these recipes, the support of healthcare professionals, and the determination to overcome.

As you embark on this transformative path, I leave you with a simple yet powerful motivation: Each blend you create, each sip you take, is a declaration of your unwavering commitment to your well-being. Let it be your daily ritual, a reminder that you are resilient, and that, together with nature's healing gifts, you are unstoppable. With every glass raised to health and vitality, you are taking back control, one delicious, nutritious, and healing sip at a time.

Made in the USA
Las Vegas, NV
22 December 2023

83449413R00030